P.S.

I LOVE ME

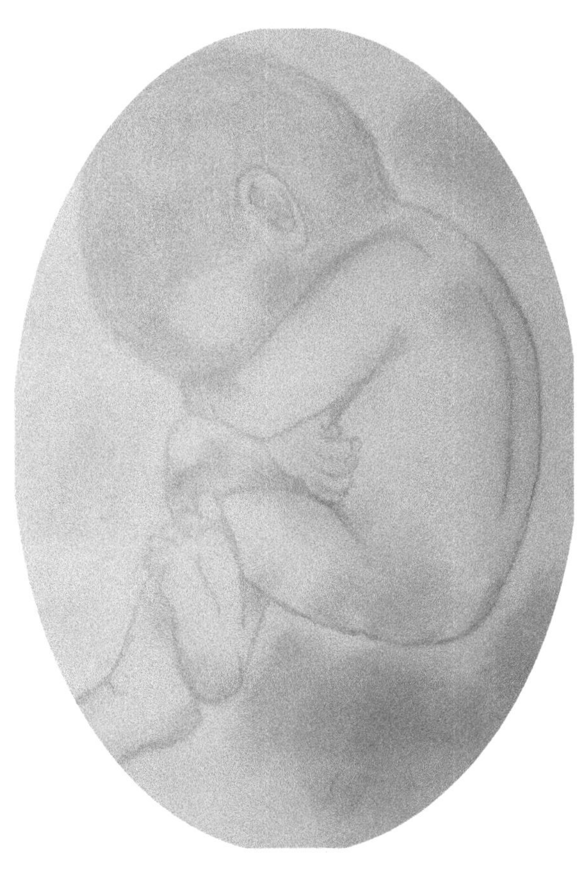

First Printing: 2014

ISBN 978-1-326-07618-4

Lulu.com

Context

For those that have loved and lost.

For those that have never loved themselves.

For those that cant find there way home.

For those that have lost themselves in the harsh reality's of life.

For those that have been taken from eating disorders.

For those that considered suicide and self harm.

For those that never put themselves first.

For those that are on the road to happiness.

Life is the only game that doesn't come with rules. When you are brought into this beautiful horror you don't receive an instruction book. Am so proud and honoured that I have a wonderful mother that told me all the rules I need to know to live my life.

"Don't do to others what you wouldn't want done to you." "Know what is right from wrong." "Always make sure that you are your first priority, your happiness should come first before anyone else's."

These small words were my stepping stones into the spiritual world. When it comes to life I believe what ever you put out into the world you shall receive back. I've had an equal amount of great and horrid experiences so far in life. My deepest thoughts are all here in black and white and hopefully it will give you a glimpse of what I've been through and how it has affected me.

The hardest part of my life would've been between the ages of 11-16. I was terribly depressed and unsatisfied with what life had given to me. What most don't know about me was that my self esteem was incredibly low. If I never had my mum there to hold me and speak kind, honest words, a life of bulimia nervosa, self harm and possibly suicide would have stolen me from her.

There are so many children that have eating disorders due to the amount of pressure put on us to look good in size and skin.

Who are you to tell me what I should look like? Who are you to tell me what I should wear? Who are you to even have an opinion? Why do we do this to ourselves and others?

How disgusting is it to put this into little girls and boys minds? All they want is to be themselves and make friends, but instead they are constantly thinking about how they appear to others. When their next meal is and how scared they are of eating it. How "disgusting and vile" they look and wishing they didn't even want to live?

But hey, I guess "that's life".

The Old Me

Whilst I'm terribly depressed in this dark, silent room,

Somehow this aggression turns into an even deeper depression.

Now I have so many emotions that I cannot explain
….why I suffer in all this hate and pain.

Because I know in the morning I will regain… the dark feelings I have,

and the strain.

Numbers, figures flying across my head, because I don't know who I'm supposed to be…

I really don't wanna be this type of me!

They tell me to get over it…tomorrow will be a better day…

To be honest, I just wanna sit on the dock of the bay,

because my days feel like years and my years feel like eternity…

What am I supposed to do… sit here in this jealousy?

Jealous of those that wake up in the morning, look in the mirror and love what they see.

That has someone to hold...has someone to love…has someone to say your beautiful in every way.

These days turned into hours, hours turned in to minutes.

I woke up that day feeling refreshed.

I was so blessed that I found the address of the doors of happiness.

This was the end…

I can finally walk into that place we call a world, leaving the extra baggage behind.

I am not designed to fit your checklist of what a "woman" is supposed to look like…

KEEP YOUR UNKIND WORDS!

I've found my peace of mind.. If you can't look past looks then…. You're clearly blind!

Fly

You never paid attention to the look in their eyes when you kissed them. That's not your fault.

Your eyes were closed, feeling the a thousand butterflies fluttering in your stomach.

Feeling there soft lips pressed up against yours.

Feeling your heart beat trying to escape from the pain due to come.

Sometimes you need to listen to your head.

Move on.

Escape.

One day you will fly with someone that actually wants you,

someone that is scared to lose you.

You will fly with someone that will accept you for the great human being that you are.

Both of you will fly.

Stupid and Naïve

Maybe I'm too stupid and naive to think that I could ever have your heart.

Maybe I'm too stupid and naive to ever think I could make me be the one that's on your mind before you close your sweet eyes.

Maybe I'm too stupid and naive to think that I even have a chance with someone like you.

Maybe I'm too stupid and naive to think that I could change you for the better.

Maybe I'm too stupid and naive to think that one day I'll be the one holding you at night whispering in your ear "goodnight".

Yeah, I think I'm too stupid and naive.

Because when I was a little girl I adored the thought of love.

That two people would do anything and everything to make the other person happy.

That two people are so committed to one another, and as that little girl grew older she still loved the idea of being in love, until it came…

Now this little girls dream are crushed and bruised,

because now she only sees love as a sickness.

A disease that hits you like a ton of bricks and without knowing, attacks your blood stream and your soul.

A disease that eats you alive and makes you weak.

That little girl inside me is crying, crying tears of disappointment.

Welcome Back x

The best and most beautiful things in the world cannot be seen or even touched - they must be felt with the heart.

You are the art.

Don't you dare tear yourself apart.

Ripping away the "ugly" from your pulchritudinous body.

Don't be a copy, of every other thin legged, supple lipped, big busted, media lusted women.

Don't be cheating yourself at the life you have to live.

Deny others access to all that you have to give.

Outlive the ugly in this society.

One step out of the door, I know you can feel your anxiety.

Are you perfect enough?

Yes indeed you are!

You've come so far. You are more than what you think you are.

Now open up that spiritual jar, throw away the negativity.

You are no longer in captivity.

You are free.

You've found the key,

To everlasting acceptance.

So pick yourself up beautiful, it's crucial that you stop being so critical about your self-worth.

Celebrate the rebirth of you.

Welcome back. x

This dark room has me in captivity.

These walls whisper to me.

This floor is like a magnet to my feet, that feel like they weigh a ton.

"Someone please pull the trigger of that gun".

As I stagger down the stairs, I can almost feel the sliver blades.

Cutting my skin, blowing up my soul like grenades.

When I turned 18 I fell for an unworthy soul, a soul that didn't deserve my time, my heart or my energy. I slowly noticed I was losing myself within the toxicity where the new arrivals of demons as well as the familiar faces laid thoughtlessly. These poems and quotes mean a great deal to me, as in this period of time I felt like a burden, as if I was unwanted. I felt like I was that little girl again, looking in the mirror at myself and thinking "what a piece of unworthy shit!" So many flaws were brought to the surface. So many imperfections were painted on my skin. Within that period of time I self harmed 3 times, due to a lack of courage and self respect. A year before this I came out to my mum that I was gay. I felt like a disappointment to not only my mother but to myself…

I gradually started to love myself for who I truly am. This made me happy, so what's the big deal?

-If society has a problem with the way you are, look to family: when I think of family, I think of support, comfort and acceptance. If family has a problem with the way you are then there is one more option that will never let you down.

Look to yourself.

The only true acceptance you can receive is from yourself. Accept yourself for who you are and how you live your life. If society, family or any other source of life doesn't like it at least you've got yourself. I guarantee you won't let yourself down.

I am so grateful and lucky I have my guardian angel (mother) and my friends, as well as myself, to hold me up.-

I love myself

The worthlessness which is written down on printer paper with blue ink

I sit there and watch it burn away the empty worded letters and memories that make my heart weak…

Although the words "I love myself" would roll off my tongue with pride and belief, it's now come to a struggle to get such words/lies out. They feel like foreign words to me because I no longer understand the sentence.

"I LOVE MYSELF"

Victim of a Foolish Heart

Why do we feel that we can mend our hearts with those that are heartless?

Why do we always end up being a victim of a foolish heart?

No Longer

Scratched and scuffed,

Detached from humanity,

Cuffed to the darkness that lies within your soul.

Imprisoned by the power of your benighted mind,

Restricted to the light, that teases you from the outside of your orbs.

You have developed this
indifferent attitude toward the suffering of others because once you cared too much.

No one ever had gratitude for what you've sacrificed.

Oblivious to the fever, the discomfort, the sickness and the misery they gave you.

Send that malaise back special delivery with a hand written note;

"You no longer own my soul, my heart.

You no longer serve me

R.I.P you're dead to me."

Take back the key, open up the door and run free.

Go on a soul finding spree, because quite frankly you're starting to look at the world blankly and you don't deserve to be anything less than happy.

Not Good Enough For You.

I tried, and tried! I tried my best for you, to show you that … I loved you. It wasn't good enough.

My heart wrote poems for you. My heart wrote poems about you. It wasn't good enough.

It wasn't love at first sight. But I loved you at your darkest.

The darkness came over you, but I never left you.

You will never know that I would come home and cry in the corner of the room, because of you.

Because of you! I lost my smile.

Because of you! I lost my temper with friends as I would stick up for you.

Because of you! I over-thought.

Because of you!

Because of you! Because of fucking you!

Maybe you didn't mean to rip out the veins of my heart. And yeah maybe you didn't mean to call out the green eyed monster which slept inside of me.

You said you wanted to be with me, so why was you in such a rush to give me away?

I AM NOT A CHARITY CASE! I AM A HUMAN BEING WITH FEELINGS SO PLEASE TREAT ME LIKE ONE!

I can't get mad at you because this is life.

Life will bring you up to the highest of heights and drop you.

Yes! I will always love you. But I'll never forget the pain I was suffering in silence.

I'll never forget the worthless feeling I would get.

I'll never forget how I felt so unappreciated.

But now it's time for me to find someone that will appreciate all the things I do for them.

Someone that will laugh at all my jokes, even if their cheesy.

We will look at each other with a smile and tell ourselves "how did we get like this?"

Yeah. I saw a future with you, it was so clear.... But clearly to you that was just a blur.

-Everyone has had a chance to see you. Yet I still haven't got that opportunity to just walk past you like you are just a bundle of leaves. Maybe someone knows that am not strong enough to do so. So they are waiting for me to create that strong energy that I need.-

More and more of us are taking less and less responsibility for our own mental and emotional well being. No one can hurt you, but you can use people to hurt yourself. Once you see that it's you who hurts yourself, not the other person who hurts you, you are halfway home. The next step is for you to accept that what was is no longer.
Detach yourself from the things that don't serve you, but never detach yourself from your emotions. Emotions are the one thing that lets you know that you're still alive.

Protect yourself from evil and poisonous people.
Unfortunately you cannot protect yourself from sadness without protecting yourself from happiness.
Don't think of happiness as a dependency it's a decision and if you want to be happy you need to make that decision.

-One of the biggest but natural weaknesses is giving advice but not even taking your own.-

"The worst than other days" feels like everybody tries their hardest to lower your self esteem to achieve the best you can or even do at least something right.-

-Always make sure you are your first priority because at the end of the day, when you lay your head on your pillow, you are left with yourself and the good or bad energy you have released throughout the day.-

You have a guest

It comes knocking at the door with no invitation. Not even the slightest warning, holds you so tight to take over every open and hidden part of you, whilst filling your arteries with substandard destructive pleasures and fantasies.

Sooner or later finding yourself drained and deleted from reality because when you wake up from your delusion you realise your existence is not as satisfying as in your dreams.

When you try to redeem yourself, your inner soul screams because your mind, body and heart aren't playing as a team. Your happiness is frequently buffering, steadily making no progress, feeling your heart beating out of your chest. Energy levels and thoughts are giving you more stress.

It comes with no warning or invite and lays there until you're strong and not so naive to respect yourself and show it to the door.

Moon Child

High self esteem is something I have on some days. Some days I leave my self esteem with those that don't think before they speak, Or those who think am perfectly fine. So they feel the need to open their mouths to say words that echo throughout my mind and translate in my language. **"Worthless"**

Some days I will walk around with a "content"smile on my face, but let the truth be told that inside there are a thousand demons whispering a wrangle of hatred. These demons strip me naked… from my so called greatness… without purpose or direction feeling like everything I do is aimless… With this hatred…I can get completely wasted with mates and look happy, just because I have painted… a permitted smile...

I am the moon child.

Guardian Angel (mother)

I look for her welcoming sweet fragrance.
The aggravating sound of her locksmith keys at the door.
Every now and then the leeches and demons come to play some more,
But I never get dragged offshore.
I could never ask for more.
She holds me up to the blazing light and looks at all the scratches, scuffs along with the deepest cracks
There's no need for her to analyse me because she knows me.
She knows what is missing and what is broken.
She fills the cracks with her words like glue,
Polishes out the scuffs
And
Gently buffers out the scratches.
Her aim is to make me shine again and bring back my self-worth.
It's never an overnight process,
But the day will come when she holds me up once again to the light and all of that looking after and hard work would have paid off.
The scratches, scuffs along with the deepest cracks will be no longer.
I shall return and share all of the guarding, love and

wisdom back to her and others that are at arms length.

Today

In today's world loyalty, acceptance, inner love and romance is so hard to find.

People are too busy feeding there temptations like a savage, drooling constantly over the bait, which walks on every street of every corner.

Short, tall, fat, thin, black, white, man, woman, gay, straight, bi, trans-

Who made these labels?

Why should each person have a label for the way they look or what they are?

I am sure our blood is all the same…

"Definitions belong to the definers, not the defined."

"People are too complicated to have simple labels."

People are constantly looking at other people to pick out there flaws. Loving that thin legged, "perfect faced" woman, but not loving themselves.

Romance died a long time ago when we stopped using our imaginations and became lazy minded. The thought of a candle lit dinner under a thousand stars was to much work… Well that's after you've got their love.

What else is there to prove?

The fact that you've only spent 3 days in their company, and you can come back to me and tell me about their affection, like you have known them for more than 3 months.

The way they looked at you like you was the most delicate creature on the planet.

The way they wasn't scared to look at your wounded body.

The way they made you feel like they was interested in every little aspect of you.

The way they tried to soothe your open cuts.

The way you told me like I haven't done any of that since the day I met you...

You said you spoke about me... "Oh what did you say?"

that I was the only one that could make your waters rock like the ocean of the"Drake Passage".

That I can make your legs have an outburst of spasms.... that I can make your eyes roll back so you can see that gentle heart you claim to have.

You never told him that I was the only person that held your hand when your demons lay recklessly in the center of your mind.

That I was the only one that bought you flowers..... I was the only one that wrote you endless poems till my heart was content.

I was the only one that held you tight and told you I loved you.

I was the only on that you said you were lucky to have in your life, every minute of every fucking day..

That I was "your strength, your fucking life saver and your everything.

That I was the only one that wiped you bleeding wrists and gripped and guarded you though the night…..

And for the last time

This is why I believe am nothing to you

I'm not your everything

I'm not your strength

Nor am I your life saver

I'm just a human that loves you… but clearly you're obviously to busy to recognize…

Because if you did... I wouldn't feel this way and it wouldn't have ended.

I constantly feel like I need to prove more to you… but then again, what else more is there to prove.

When they are truly gone, you see them for what everyone else did. You undress that blind fold that was covering your sight. You remove the harsh words that are written all over your body, from head to toe. From mind to soul, in a matter of time you shall be re born. Well, let's hope for the best...

I think of life like a book, a book full of chapters. This book was just one chapter in my life, which felt like years when it was only a couple of months. I've accepted this chapter in my life, learnt many lessons, found my soul that was lost, revitalized myself and learnt to love myself again.

Someone very special has entered my life and has helped me start a new happier chapter. Someone that pulled me up from that deep puddle in which I fell in. someone that has the strength to pick up my heart from my shoulders and placed it ever so gently back into my chest.

- I stole her from you physically,
Whilst you stole her emotionally.
What gives you the right to draw tears
From her precious eyes?
She put her all into you,
I put my all into her.
You abused her mind,
I consoled her soul.
You ripped her heart from her chest,
I snatched it from your selfish hands
And put it back where it belonged.
You caused her pain,
Even after you weren't around.
Now she's damaged.
She can't let me in anymore,
Because you damaged her.
But don't you worry.
I'm gonna fix her.
I will make her believe that she is beautiful.
I will open up them pretty eyes,
And make her stand up and say to herself,
"I am amazing".
You failed,
But on my life, I will not.-

-Bethany Clarke-

And on her life she did not fail at all.

I used to have a blood diamond: it was so beautiful to the eye, but so ugly inside. I wanted it but it was deadly to me. So I had to throw it away and get myself a Pink Star diamond. I picked so carefully to get the best. I don't regret anything. Its beauty is one in a million, inside and out. It's the one designed for me

-Raeven Leigh Winter-

P.S. I LOVE ME

www.ingramcontent.com/pod-product-compliance
Ingram Content Group UK Ltd.
Pitfield, Milton Keynes, MK11 3LW, UK
UKHW020228250726
13967UKWH00001B/246

9 781326 076184